Clothes We Wear

Katie Peters

GRL Consultant Diane Craig,
Certified Literacy Specialist

Lerner Publications ◆ Minneapolis

Lerner Publications
An imprint of Lerner Publishing Group, Inc.
241 First Avenue North
Minneapolis, MN 55401 USA

For reading levels and more information, look up this title at www.lernerbooks.com.

Main body text set in Memphis Pro 24/39
Typeface provided by Linotype.

Photo Acknowledgments
The images in this book are used with the permission of: © Evgeniy Skripnichenko/iStockphoto, p. 3; © Rawpixel/iStockphoto, pp. 4–5; © monkeybusinessimages/iStockphoto, pp. 6–7, 16 (stripes); © Dobrila Vignjevic/iStockphoto, pp. 8–9; © Fotoluminate LLC/Shutterstock Images, pp. 10–11, 16 (hood); © iofoto/Shutterstock Images, pp. 12–13, 16 (pants); © JGalione/iStockphoto, pp. 14–15.

Front cover: © monkeybusinessimages/iStockphoto

Library of Congress Cataloging-in-Publication Data

Names: Peters, Katie, author.
Title: Clothes we wear / Katie Peters ; GRL Consultant Diane Craig, Certified Literacy Specialist.
Description: Minneapolis, MN : Lerner Publications, [2023] | Series: My world (Pull ahead readers - nonfiction) | Audience: Ages 4–7 | Audience: Grades K–1 | Summary: "This nonfiction title engages emerging readers with the types of clothes people wear. Pairs with the fiction book, Khalil's Clothes"— Provided by publisher.
Identifiers: LCCN 2022006205 (print) | LCCN 2022006206 (ebook) | ISBN 9781728475943 (library binding) | ISBN 9781728478869 (paperback) | ISBN 9781728483740 (ebook)
Subjects: LCSH: Clothing and dress—Juvenile literature.
Classification: LCC GT518 .P45 2023 (print) | LCC GT518 (ebook) | DDC 391—dc23/eng/20211130

LC record available at https://lccn.loc.gov/2022006205
LC ebook record available at https://lccn.loc.gov/2022006206

Manufactured in the United States of America
1 – CG – 12/15/22

Table of Contents

Clothes We Wear.......4

Did You See It? 16

Index...................16

Clothes We Wear

We all wear clothes.

I like my shirt.

It has stripes.

I wear my dress.

It has flowers.

I like my hoodie.

It keeps me warm.

I wear pants.
They are black.

What do you like to wear?

What is your favorite piece of clothing?

Did You See It?

hood

pants

stripes

Index

dress, 9

flowers, 9

hoodie, 11

pants, 13

shirt, 7

stripes, 7